TypeScript

If you have any questions, comments, or feedback about this book, I would love to hear from you.

Please feel free to reach out to me via email:

Email: ec.books.contact@gmail.com

Table of Contents

Info

The code in this guide was tested with ECMAScript 2022 version.

There may be certain syntax, code constructs, or concepts that are not explained in some topics, but they will be discussed later to avoid confusing the reader.

This book is written in a minimalistic style and follows a logical flow of topics, allowing you to write programs quickly without unnecessary delays.

Prerequisites

JavaScript - Proficiency in the JavaScript language is a must, look for the book at amazon. https://www.amazon.com/dp/B0CQD3SHY4

HTML - Preferred, but it's not mandatory.

CSS - Preferred, but it's not mandatory.

Introduction

TypeScript is a free and open-source programming language developed by Microsoft.

TypeScript is a statically typed superset of JavaScript that adds optional static typing to the language. It is designed for large-scale application development, offering features such as interfaces, classes, enums, and modules to help developers write more robust and maintainable code.

TypeScript is a superset of JavaScript, which means that anything you can do in JavaScript is also valid TypeScript code. TypeScript code gets transpiled into JavaScript, and the resulting JavaScript code is what actually runs in browsers or other JavaScript environments.

Static Typing

JavaScript Challenge: JavaScript is dynamically typed, meaning that variable types are determined at runtime. This can lead to runtime errors that might be difficult to catch during development.

TypeScript Solution: TypeScript introduces static typing, allowing developers to specify types for variables, function parameters, and return values. This helps catch type-related errors at compile-time, providing better code quality and tooling support.

Code Maintainability

JavaScript Challenge: In large and complex codebases, maintaining and understanding the structure of the code can be challenging.

TypeScript Solution: TypeScript's static typing, interfaces, and other features help developers express their intent more clearly, making the codebase more self-documenting and maintainable.

Development Environment

To develop with TypeScript , you'll need a code development environment.

environments:

1. Visual Studio Code (VS Code) - lightweight, free, and open-source code editor developed by Microsoft

   https://visualstudio.microsoft.com/downloads

2. Chrome or other browsers

3. Node.js https://nodejs.org/en/download

4. TypeScript

In this book, I will demonstrate the code with Visual Studio Code.

Useful Links

Typescript site - https://www.typescriptlang.org

RxJS - https://rxjs.dev

Set up the development environment

1. Node.js and npm are essential components for building and running TypeScript applications. npm(Node Package Manager) is the default package manager for Node.js, and it allows you to install and manage packages (libraries, frameworks, tools) for your projects.

   Install - https://nodejs.org/en/download

2. Install Visual Studio Code - https://visualstudio.microsoft.com/downloads

3. Create new folder

4. Open the folder inside visual studio code, File -> Open Folder

5. Open Terminal View -> Terminal

6. Install TypeScript, enter this command in the terminal:

   ```
   npm install -g typescript
   ```

   The command installs TypeScript globally on your system using npm

   Packages can be installed globally (accessible from any project) using the -g flag, or locally (for a specific project) without the flag.

   PROBLEMS   OUTPUT   DEBUG CONSOLE   TERMINAL   PORTS

   ```
   PS C:\1\TypeScriptEldar> npm install -g typescript

   added 1 package in 1s
   ```

7. Enter command: `npm init -y`

   That will create a package.json file with default values. The -y flag stands for "yes" and automatically accepts all default configurations

   The package.json file is a crucial part of Node.js projects. It contains metadata about the project and its dependencies, and it can also include scripts, configuration, and other details

8. Create a 'src' folder and, within it, create a file named 'app.ts.' Enter the following code into the file:

```typescript
function sayHello(name: string): void {
    console.log(`Hello, ${name}!`);
}
sayHello("TypeScript");
```

9. Enter command: `tsc --init`

   This will create a tsconfig.json file with default settings

   tsconfig.json is a configuration file used in TypeScript projects to specify compiler options and settings. When you have a TypeScript project, you use tsc (TypeScript Compiler) to transpile TypeScript code into JavaScript.

10. Add/Edit those lines inside the tsconfig.ts file:

```json
"outDir": "./dist"
"sourceMap": true
"target": "es2022"
```

   The **outDir** property specifies the directory where the compiled JavaScript files will be placed.

   The **sourceMap**: true option is essential for generating source maps, which are necessary for debugging TypeScript code in VS Code.

   The **target** specifies the ECMAScript version to which TypeScript will transpile your code. In this case, it indicates that the generated JavaScript should adhere to the ECMAScript 2022 (ES12) standard.

11. Enter command: `tsc`

   tsc command Compile the TypeScript code into JavaScript using the TypeScript compiler (tsc)

12. Enter command: `node dist/app.js`

   Node command will run you code

```
PS C:\1\TypeScriptEldar> node dist/app.js
Hello, TypeScript!
```

package.json

```json
{
  "name": "typescripteldar",
  "version": "1.0.0",
  "description": "",
  "main": "index.js",
  "type": "module",
  "dependencies": {
  },
  "devDependencies": {},
  "scripts": {
    "test": "echo \"Error: no test specified\" && exit 1"
  },
  "keywords": [],
  "author": "",
  "license": "ISC"
}
```

tsconfig.json

```json
{
  "compilerOptions": {
    "target": "ES2022",
    "module": "ES2022",
    "sourceMap": true,
    "esModuleInterop": true,
    "forceConsistentCasingInFileNames": true,
    "strict": true,
    "skipLibCheck": true,
    "outDir": "./dist",
    "experimentalDecorators": true,
    "moduleResolution": "node",
  }
}
```

Configure the vs code to run the code

1. Press the button

2. Press the button

3. Press create a launch.json file

4. Press Node.js

5. Now enter the launch.json file and add/edit those lines

```
"program": "${workspaceFolder}/dist/app.js"
"preLaunchTask": "tsc: watch - tsconfig.json"
```

6. Press the green button   ▷ Launch Pro ∨

PROBLEMS   OUTPUT   DEBUG CONSOLE   TERMINAL   PORTS

C:\Program Files\nodejs\node.exe .\dist\app.js
Hello, TypeScript!

Project Explorer

The **app.js.map** file is a source map file generated by TypeScript compiler (tsc). Source maps are files that contain information about the original TypeScript code structure and how it maps to the generated JavaScript code. They are used to help debug the original TypeScript code in the browser or other JavaScript runtime environments.

```
{"version":3,"file":"app.js","sourceRoot":"","sources":["../app.ts"],"names":[],"mappings":";AAAA,SAAS,QAAQ,CAAC,IAAY;IAC1B,OAAO,CAAC,GAAG,CAAC,UAAU,IAAI,GAAG,CAAC,CAAC;AACjC,CAAC;AAED,QAAQ,CAAC,aAAa,CAAC,CAAC"}
```

The **package-lock.json** file is used by npm (Node Package Manager) to lock down the version of every package and its dependencies that are installed in a project.

The **node_modules** folder is a directory created by npm (Node Package Manager) when you install dependencies for a Node.js project. It contains all the packages and their dependencies that your project relies on.

- ∨ .vscode
  - {} launch.json
- ∨ dist
  - JS app.js
  - JS app.js.map
- > node_modules
- ∨ src
  - TS app.ts
- {} package-lock.json
- {} package.json
- TS tsconfig.json

Auto Compile

Configure the vs code to automatically compile the ts code after saving changes

1. Press ctrl + shift + b

2. Press the wheel button of the tsc: watch line
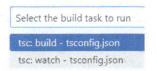

   Now you have tasks.json file

3. Press ctrl + shift + b

4. Make change in you code and save

5. Press

   Vs code compiled the ts code for you automatically

Configure the vs code to run the code in chrome instead the debug console

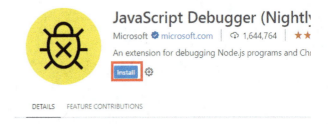

Variable Types

TypeScript introduces static typing to JavaScript, providing a way to catch potential errors during development and improve code quality.

Primitive Types

number: Represents numeric values.

```
let age: number = 30;
```

string: Represents textual data.

```
let firstName: string = "Eldar";
```

boolean: Represents true or false values.

```
let isActive: boolean = true;
```

bigint: Represents arbitrary precision integers.

```
let num: bigint = 1n;
```

Enforce data type

TypeScript checks and enforces data types at compile-time, before the code is executed. If there are mismatches or inconsistencies in data types, TypeScript will throw an error during the compilation process.

```
let myNum: number = 1;
myNum = "str"; // Type error: Type 'string' is not
        // assignable to type 'number'.
```

Union type

A union type allows a variable to have one of multiple specified types. It is denoted by the use of the pipe (|) symbol between the types.

```
let num: number | string;
num = 1;
num = '2';
num = true // error: Type 'boolean' is not assignable to
        // type 'string | number'
```

null/undefined

null and **undefined**: Represent absence of value.

In TypeScript, if you want to allow a variable to hold either null or undefined (or both), you can declare the variable as having a union type that includes null and/or undefined. This is often referred to as making the variable "nullable" or "optional."

```
let num: number | null = 5;

num = null;

let num2: number | undefined = 5;

let num3: number | null | undefined = 5;
num3 = null;
num3 = undefined;
```

Explicit Type/Implicit Type

Variables can have explicit or implicit types based on how you declare and initialize them. These terms refer to whether you explicitly specify the type of a variable or let TypeScript infer the type automatically.

Explicit Type

When you explicitly specify the type of a variable, you provide TypeScript with information about the expected type. You do this by appending a colon (:) followed by the type after the variable name.

```
let myNum: number = 1;
```

Implicit Type (Type Inference)

When you don't explicitly specify the type, TypeScript uses type inference to determine the type based on the value assigned to the variable.

```
let str = "Hello"; // TypeScript infers the type as string
let num = 1;       // TypeScript infers the type as number
let bool = true;   // TypeScript infers the type as boolean
```

any

The any type is a dynamic type that allows values of any type to be assigned to variables of this type. It essentially turns off TypeScript's type checking for variables of this type.

```
let dynamicValue: any = 1;
dynamicValue = 'a'
```

unknown

The unknown type is similar to any, but it is more type-safe. Variables of type unknown require explicit type checking before performing operations on them.

```
let dynamicValue: unknown = 1;
dynamicValue = 'a'
```

```
let var1: any = 1;
let var2: unknown = 1;

var1.func(); // runtime error - var1.func is not a function
var2.func(); // compile error - 'var2' is of type 'unknown'
```

With var1 being of type any, TypeScript allows any property or method access without type checking. The func() method call will not result in a compile-time error, even though the actual type of var1 is not known until runtime. This flexibility comes at the cost of reduced type safety.

With var2 being of type unknown, TypeScript requires you to perform a type check or use a type assertion before accessing properties or calling methods. Attempting to directly call func() on var2 results in a compile-time error, enforcing type safety.

```
if (typeof var2 === 'object' && var2 !== null
        && typeof (var2 as any).func === 'function') {
   (var2 as any).func(); // Type assertion to any
}
```

never

The never type is a type that represents values that never occur. If a variable is explicitly annotated as never, it means that the variable should never be assigned any value.

```
let x: never;
x = 1;//error: Type number is not assignable to type never.
```

Type assertion/Cast

Type assertion in TypeScript is a way to tell the compiler that you, as a developer, know more about the type of a value than TypeScript does. It is like a type cast in other languages, but it doesn't actually change the type of the variable at runtime, it's just a way to inform the TypeScript compiler about the variable's type.

Risks of Type Assertion: Type assertion essentially tells the TypeScript compiler to trust the developer's judgment. If misused or if the asserted type is incorrect, it can lead to runtime errors. It's crucial to be confident about the type before using type assertion. Whenever possible, consider using type checks or refining types through conditional statements to avoid the need for type assertion.

Angle Bracket Syntax

```
let value: any = "Eldar";
let strLength: number = (<string>value).length;
```

In this example, we use the angle bracket syntax (<string>value) to assert that value is of type string. This allows us to access the length property without causing a compilation error.

As Operator Syntax

The **as** keyword is another way to perform type assertion.

```
let value: any = "Eldar";
let strLength: number = (value as string).length;
```

Array

Arrays are similar to those in JavaScript but with the added benefit of static typing. You can define arrays using the standard array syntax, and TypeScript allows you to specify the type of elements within the array.

```
let numbers: number[] = [1, 2, 3];
let strings: string[] = ["a", "b", "c"];
```

Another way to declare an array is by using the Array keyword:

```
let numbers: Array<number> = [1, 2, 3];
let strings: Array<string> = ["a", "b", "c"];
```

Tuple

A tuple is a finite ordered list of elements that each have a specific type. Unlike arrays, tuples allow you to specify the type for each element individually, making them more flexible in certain situations.

```
let user: [string, number] = ["Eldar", 30];

console.log(user[0]); // "Eldar"
console.log(user[1]); // 30
```

Inference

If you initialize a tuple without explicitly specifying its type, TypeScript will infer the types based on the provided values:

```
let user = ["Eldar", 30];
```

Tuple Destructuring

You can destructure tuples to assign their elements to individual variables:

```
let user: [string, number] = ["Eldar", 30];

let [firstName, age] = user;

console.log(firstName); // "Eldar"
console.log(age); // 30
```

Union type

You can use union types within tuples to allow elements to have more than one possible type.

```
let user: [string | null, number | string] = ["Eldar", 30];
```

enum

enums (short for enumerations) allow you to define a set of named numeric constants. Enums can make your code more readable and maintainable by giving meaningful names to values.

```typescript
enum Country {
    Israel,
    USA,
    UK
}

let myCountry: Country = Country.Israel;

console.log(myCountry);   // Outputs: 0
console.log(Country.USA); // Outputs: 1
console.log(Country.UK);  // Outputs: 2
```

In this example, the Country enum is defined with 3 members: Israel, USK, and UK. If you don't assign explicit values to enum members, TypeScript assigns them numeric values starting from 0.

You can also explicitly set values for enum members:

```typescript
enum Country {
    Israel = 5,
    USA = "us",
    UK = 1
}

console.log(Country.Israel); // Outputs: 5
console.log(Country.USA); // Outputs: "us"
console.log(Country.UK); // Outputs: 1
```

```typescript
enum Country {
    Israel = 5,
    USA,
    UK
}
console.log(Country.Israel); // Outputs: 5
console.log(Country.USA); // Outputs: 6
console.log(Country.UK); // Outputs: 7
```

type

A type alias is a way to create a custom name for a type. It allows you to define complex or repeated types using a single name, improving code readability and maintainability. You can use type aliases to represent any valid TypeScript type, including primitives, unions, intersections, and more.

```typescript
type Id = number;
type FirstName = string;

let userId: Id = 1;
let userName: FirstName = "Eldar";
```

Intersection types (&)

Intersection types allow you to combine multiple types into a single type that has all the features of each of the individual types. The syntax for an intersection type is denoted by the & (ampersand) symbol.

```typescript
// Define two types representing different aspects of an object
type Printable = {
  print: () => void;
};

type Loggable = {
  log: () => void;
};

// Combine the two types using an intersection type
type PrintableAndLoggable = Printable & Loggable;

// Create an object that has both print and log methods
const myObject: PrintableAndLoggable = {
  print: () => console.log("Printing..."),
  log: () => console.log("Logging..."),
};

myObject.print(); // Output: Printing...
myObject.log();   // Output: Logging...
```

By using the & operator, we create a new type called PrintableAndLoggable, which includes both the print and log methods. The resulting type, PrintableAndLoggable, can be used to describe objects that satisfy both the Printable and Loggable requirements.

Non-Null Assertion Operator (!)

The non-null assertion operator (!) is used to assert to the TypeScript compiler that a value is indeed not null or undefined. It tells TypeScript to treat the expression as non-nullable, even if the type checker might not be able to guarantee it.

While the non-null assertion operator can be helpful in certain situations, it should be used with caution, as it essentially tells TypeScript to trust you about the non-nullability of a value without providing any runtime safety. If you use the non-null assertion operator incorrectly, it may lead to runtime errors.

```
let str: string | undefined;

let username1: string = str;
// error: Type 'string | undefined' is not assignable to
// type 'string'. Type 'undefined' is not assignable
// to type 'string'

// Using the non-null assertion operator
let username2: string = str!;
```

In this example, str is of type string | undefined. By using the non-null assertion operator (str!), you're telling TypeScript that you're confident str is not undefined at this point. However, if str is actually undefined at runtime, you'll get a runtime error.

Function

In TypeScript, functions can be explicitly typed to provide information about the types of their parameters and return values. This helps catch potential errors at compile-time and provides better code documentation.

```typescript
function add(x: number, y: number): number {
    return x + y;
}
```

In this example, the add function takes two parameters (x and y), both of type number, and returns a value of type number.

arrow function with a defined type

```typescript
const add = (a: number, b: number): number => a + b;

let result: number = add(1, 2);

console.log(result) // 3
```

void

The void type is used to indicate that a function does not return any value. This is typically the case for functions that perform some action but do not produce a meaningful result.

```typescript
function Print(): void {

    console.log("Hello");

}
```

Optional Parameters

Optional parameters marked by adding ? after their name

```
function Print(x: number, y?: number) {

    if (y) {
        console.log(y);
    } else {
        console.log(x);
    }
}

Print(1);    // 1
Print(1, 2); // 2
```

In this example, the print parameter is marked as optional by adding ? after its name.

When you have both optional and non-optional parameters in a function, the optional parameters must be placed at the end of the parameter list. This is because, in JavaScript, when you call a function, arguments are assigned to parameters based on their positions.

never

A function with a return type of never is a function that is expected to never complete normally or return a value. The never type is used to represent functions that throw exceptions, enter into infinite loops, or have other behaviors that prevent them from returning a value or completing successfully.

```
function throwError(message: string): never {
    throw new Error(message);
}

try {
    throwError("This is an error message");
} catch (error) {

}
```

```
function infiniteLoop(): never {
    while (true) {
        // Code that never exits the loop
    }
}

// This function will never return
infiniteLoop();
```

Objects

Object Literal Type

You can define an object type using an object literal syntax:

```
let user: { name: string, age: number } = {
    name: "Eldar",
    age: 30
};

user.age = "a"; // error: Type 'string' is not assignable
            // to type 'number'
```

type keyword

You can use the type keyword to create a type alias for an object type:

```
type User = { name: string, age: number };

let user: User = { name: "Eldar", age: 30 };

console.log(user.name) // "Eldar"
```

Optional parameter

You can make properties of an object type optional by using the **?** modifier. This allows you to create object types where certain properties may or may not be present.

```typescript
//without optional parameter
let user: { name: string, age: number } = { name: "Eldar"};
// error: Property 'age' is missing in type { name: string}
// but required in type { name: string, age: number }


//with optional parameter
let user2: { name: string, age?: number } ={name: "Eldar"};
```

class

When you declare a class property without initializing it in the constructor or providing a default value, TypeScript assumes the property could be undefined or null.

```
class User {
    public firstName: string;
    // error: Property 'firstName' has no initializer and
    // is not definitely assigned in the constructor
}
```

To resolve this issue, you have a few options:

Use a Default Property Value:

```
class User {
    public firstName: string = ";
}
```

Use the Definite Assignment Assertion (!):

```
class User {
    public firstName!: string;
}

let user: User = new User();
console.log(user.firstName); // undefined
```

Use the ? syntax:

```
class User {
    public firstName?: string;//equal to string | undefined;
}
```

28

Initialize Properties in the Constructor:

```
class User {

  public firstName: string;

  constructor(firstName: string) {
    this.firstName = firstName;
  }
}
```

Access Modifiers

Access modifiers are keywords that control the visibility and accessibility of class members (properties and methods). Using access modifiers helps enforce encapsulation, ensuring that the internal implementation details of a class are not unnecessarily exposed and promoting better code organization and maintenance.

Public: The public access modifier is the default if no modifier is specified. Public members are accessible from anywhere, both within the class and outside of it.

Private: The private access modifier restricts access to the member only within the declaring class. It is not accessible from outside the class or from derived classes.

Protected: The protected access modifier is similar to private, but it allows access within the declaring class and its derived classes.

```
class User {

  public firstName?: string
  private lastName?: string

  protected print(): void {
    console.log("Hello");
  }
}
```

Parameter properties

Parameter properties provide a shorthand syntax to declare and initialize class properties directly within the constructor parameter list.

Declare property inside the constructor signature:

```
class User {
    constructor(public firstName?: string) {
        this.firstName = firstName;
    }
}
```

readonly

The readonly modifier is used to make a property or variable immutable, meaning its value cannot be changed after it has been initialized. This is particularly useful when you want to ensure that certain values remain constant throughout the life of an object.

```
class User {
    public readonly id?: number = 1;
}

let user: User = new User();
user.id = 2; // error: Cannot assign to 'id' because it is        // a read-only property
```

While both const and readonly contribute to immutability, the key distinction is that const applies to variables, and readonly applies to properties or elements within objects or arrays. readonly is enforced only at compile-time, while const is enforced both at compile-time and runtime. Therefore, the usage depends on the specific context and the level of immutability you want to achieve.

```
let arr: readonly number[] = [1, 2, 3];
```

Optional chaining (?.)

Optional chaining provides a concise way to access properties or elements of an object or array when there's a possibility that a property or element may be undefined or null. This helps to avoid runtime errors due to trying to access properties on undefined or null values.

Object Properties

```
class User {
  name?: {
    first: string;
    last: string;
  };
}

const user: User = { name: { first: "Eldar", last: "Cohen" } };

// Without optional chaining
const firstNameWithoutOptionalChaining = user.name
                        && user.name.first;

// With optional chaining
const firstNameWithOptionalChaining = user.name?.first;

console.log(firstNameWithoutOptionalChaining); // "Eldar"
console.log(firstNameWithOptionalChaining);    // "Eldar"
```

```typescript
const numbers: number[] = [1, 2, 3, 4, 5];

// Without optional chaining
const thirdElementWithoutOptionalChaining =
      numbers[2] !== undefined ? numbers[2] : undefined;

// With optional chaining
const thirdElementWithOptionalChaining = numbers?.[2];

console.log(thirdElementWithoutOptionalChaining); // 3
console.log(thirdElementWithOptionalChaining);    // 3
```

Non-Null Assertion Operator (!.)

The non-null assertion operator (!.) also provides a concise way to access properties or elements of an object or array when there's a possibility that a property or element may be undefined or null.

```typescript
class User {
  name?: {
    first: string;
    last: string;
  };
}

const user: User = { name: { first: "Eldar", last: "Cohen" } };

// With  non-null assertion operator
const firstName = user.name!.first;

console.log(firstName); // "Eldar"
```

interface

An interface is a way to define a contract for the structure of an object. Interface serve as a blueprint for other classes. They cannot be instantiated directly. Interface contain properties and empty methods. Interface enforce the implementation of specified properties and methods.

```
interface IUser {
    firstName: string;
    age?: number; // Optional property
}

let user1: IUser = {
    age: 30,
};// error: Property 'firstName' is missing in type
 // { age: number } but required in type 'IUser'

let user2: IUser = {
    firstName: "Eldar",
};
```

You can make properties optional by adding a question mark (?), which means you don't have to implement them.

Function Types

Interfaces can define function types.

```
interface IMathOperation {
    (x: number, y: number): number;
}

let add: IMathOperation = (x, y) => x + y;
```

This IMathOperation interface defines a function type that takes two numbers and returns a number. The add function adheres to this interface.

implements

The implements keyword is used to declare that a class or object adheres to a particular interface.

```
interface IUser {
    firstName: string;
    print(): void;
}

class User implements IUser {
    firstName: string = '';
    print() { console.log("Hello"); };
}
```

Extending Interfaces

Interfaces can extend other interfaces to create a new one that includes the properties and methods of the extended interfaces:

```
interface IContact {
    email: string;
    phone?: string;
}

interface IUser extends IContact {
    firstName: string;
    LastName?: string;
}

class User implements IUser {
    firstName: string = '';
    email: string = '';
}

let user: IUser = new User();
```

Multiple interfaces

A class can inherit from multiple interfaces.

```
interface IContact {
    email: string;
    phone?: string;
}

interface IUser {
    firstName: string;
    LastName?: string;
}

class User implements IUser, IContact {
    firstName: string = ";
    email: string = ";
}

let user: User = new User();
```

Abstract

Abstract classes provide a way to define common functionality for a group of related classes. They cannot be instantiated directly. Abstract classes can contain abstract methods, which are methods that have no implementation in the abstract class and must be implemented by derived classes.

Abstract classes combine features of both regular classes and interfaces when using the abstract word before the property/method it enforces the implementation of specified properties and methods.

A class can only inherit from a single abstract class.

```typescript
abstract class Contact {
    email?: string = 'eldar@mail.com';
    send(): void {console.log(`Send Email ${this.email}`)};
    abstract phone: string;
    abstract print(): void;
}

class User extends Contact {
    firstName: string = '';
    phone: string = '';
    print(): void {
        console.log("Hello");
    }
}

let user: User = new User ();

user.send(); // "eldar@mail.com"
```

Decorators

Decorators are a way to add metadata or modify the behavior of classes, class members (properties and methods), and function parameters. Decorators are functions that are prefixed with the @ symbol and are applied to declarations using the @decorator syntax. There are several built-in decorators in TypeScript, and you can also create your own custom decorators. You can apply multiple decorators to the same class, property, method.

Add tsconfig.json file if needed:

```
"experimentalDecorators": true
```

Class decorator

```typescript
// Class decorator
function MyClassDecorator(target: Function) {
    // Add some logic
    console.log(target); // output: class MyClass { }
}

@MyClassDecorator
class MyClass {

}
```

Method decorator

```
// Method decorator
function MyMethodDecorator(target: any, propertyKey: string, descriptor: PropertyDescriptor) {

console.log(`target: ${JSON.stringify(target)}, propertyKey: ${propertyKey}, descriptor: ${JSON.stringify(descriptor)}`);

// Output: target: {}, propertyKey: func, descriptor:
// {"writable":true,"enumerable":false,"configurable":true}

}

class MyClass {
    @MyMethodDecorator
    func() {

    }
}
```

Parameter decorator

```
// Parameter decorator
function MyParameterDecorator(target: any,
propertyKey: string, parameterIndex: number) {

console.log(`target: ${JSON.stringify(target)}, propertyKey: ${propertyKey}, parameterIndex: ${parameterIndex}`);

//Output: target: {}, propertyKey: func, parameterIndex: 0
}

class MyClass {
    func(@MyParameterDecorator param: string) { }
}
```

Property decorator

```typescript
// Property decorator
function MyPropertyDecorator(target: any, propertyKey: string) {
  console.log(`target: ${JSON.stringify(target)}, propertyKey: ${propertyKey}`);

  // Output: target: {}, propertyKey: email
}

class MyClass {
  @MyPropertyDecorator
  email: string = 'eldar@mail.com';
}
```

Accessor decorator

```typescript
// Accessor decorator
function MyAccessorDecorator(target: any,
propertyKey: string, descriptor: PropertyDescriptor) {

console.log(`target: ${JSON.stringify(target)}, propertyKey: ${propertyKey}, descript
or: ${JSON.stringify(descriptor)}`);

// Output: target: {}, propertyKey: myProperty, descriptor: {"enumerable":false,"confi
gurable":true}
}

class MyClass {
  email: string = 'eldar@mail.com';

  @MyAccessorDecorator
  get myProperty(): string {
    return this.email;
  }
}
```

Send parameters to a decorator

To send parameters to a decorator you can create a higher-order function that returns the actual decorator. This way, the higher-order function can accept parameters, and the returned decorator will have access to those parameters.

```typescript
function MyDecorator(role: string) {

  if (role !== 'admin') {
    throw new Error(`Access denied`);
  }
  return function (target: any, propertyKey: string) {

  };
}

class MyClass {
  @MyDecorator('admin')
  func() {

  }
}
```

Generics

Generics provide a mechanism for writing code that is both flexible and type-safe. By using generics, you can create functions, classes, and interfaces that can work with a variety of data types while still ensuring type safety during compilation.

Function Generics

```
function myFunc<T>(x: T): T {
    return x;
}

let result = myFunc<string>("Hello");
// result is of type string, explicitly specified by the
// generic type argument x

let result2 = myFunc<number>(5);
// result is of type number, explicitly specified by the
// generic type argument x

let result3 = myFunc(10);
// result is of type number, explicitly specified by the
// generic type argument x
```

Array Generics

```
function toArray<T>(x: T): T[] {
    return [x];
}

let arrayResult = toArray("abc");
//arrayResult is of type string[], inferred from the x type

console.log(arrayResult) // ['abc']
```

Class Generics

```typescript
class User<T> {
  private value: T;

  constructor(value: T) {
    this.value = value;
  }

  getValue(): T {
    return this.value;
  }
}

let user = new User<number>(1);
let val = user.getValue();
```

Interface Generics

```typescript
interface IPair<T, U> {
  first: T;
  second: U;
}

let pair: IPair<string, number> = { first: "1", second: 2};
```

Constraints on Generics

You can impose constraints on generics:

```
interface ILength {
    length: number;
}

function loggingIdentity<T extends ILength>(val: T): T {
    console.log(x.length);
    return x;
}

let res = loggingIdentity({ length: 1, value: 2 });
```

The function loggingIdentity is a generic function that takes a type parameter T which extends (T extends) the Length interface. This means that the function expects its val to have a length property of type number.

```
function createPair<S, T>(v1: S, v2: T): [S, T] {
    return [v1, v2];
}

let pair1: [string, number] = createPair("hello", 1);
// pair1 is of type [string, number]

let pair2: [boolean, string] = createPair(true, "hello");
// pair2 is of type [boolean, string]
```

The createPair function is a generic function that takes two parameters of different types (S and T) and returns an array [S, T] containing these values.

Default Value

Generics can be assigned default values which apply if no other value is specified or inferred.

```
function print<T = string>(val: T): void {

}

// If T is not provided, it defaults to DefaultType string
print(1); // val is of type number
print();  // val is of type string because DefaultType is
        // string
```

Utility Types

Utility types are predefined generic types that provide common and useful transformations or operations on types. These utility types help make your type definitions more concise, readable, and maintainable.

Partial<Type>

Creates a type with all properties of the given type set to optional.

```
interface User {
    id: number;
    firstName: string;
}

type PartialUser = Partial<User>;

    // Usage
const partialUser: PartialUser = {};
```

Required<Type>

Creates a type with all properties of the given type set to required.

```typescript
interface PartialUser {
    id?: number;
    fName?: string;
}

// Usage
const user: Required<PartialUser> ={id:1, fName:"Eldar" };
```

Readonly<Type>

Creates a type with all properties of the given type set to readonly.

```typescript
interface User {
    id: number;
    firstName: string;
}

type ReadonlyUser = Readonly<User>;

// Usage
const user: ReadonlyUser = { id: 1, firstName: "Eldar" };

user.id = 2; // Error: Cannot assign to 'id' because it is
        // a read-only property.
```

Record<Keys, Type>

Creates a type with a set of properties defined by the keys of the provided type and values of the provided type.

```typescript
type Fruit = "apple" | "banana" | "orange";
type FruitCount = Record<Fruit, number>;

// Usage
const fruitCounts:FruitCount = {apple:1,banana:2,orange:3};
```

Omit<Type, Keys>

Creates a type by omitting the properties specified by the keys from the given type.

```typescript
interface IUser {
    id: number;
    firstName: string;
    age: number;
}

type UserWithoutAge = Omit<IUser, "age">;

// Usage
const userWithoutAge: UserWithoutAge =
                { id: 1, firstName: "Eldar" };
```

Exclude<Type, ExcludedUnion>

Creates a type by excluding all union members that are assignable to the second union from the first union.

```
type Numbers = 1 | 2 | 3 | 4;
type OddNumbers = Exclude<Numbers, 2 | 4>;

// Usage
const oddNumber: OddNumbers = 1; // valid
const invalidNumber: OddNumbers = 2; // Error: Type '2' is            //
not assignable to type 'OddNumbers'.
```

Extract<Type, Union>

Creates a type by extracting all union members that are assignable to the second union from the first union.

```
type Numbers = 1 | 2 | 3 | 4;
type EvenNumbers = Extract<Numbers, 2 | 4>;

// Usage
const evenNumber: EvenNumbers = 2; // valid
const invalidNumber: EvenNumbers = 1; // Error: Type '1' is//
not assignable to type 'EvenNumbers'.
```

NonNullable<Type>

Creates a type by removing null and undefined from the given type.

```
type NullableString = string | null | undefined;
type NonNullableString = NonNullable<NullableString>;

   // Usage
const nonNullableString: NonNullableString = "Hello";
```

ReturnType<Type>

Extract the return type of a function type. It takes a function type as a parameter and returns the type that represents the return value of that function.

```
type MyFunction = () => string;

type MyFunctionReturnType = ReturnType<MyFunction>;
// MyFunctionReturnType is string
```

Parameters<Type>

Extract the parameter types of a function type. It takes a function type as a parameter and returns a tuple type representing the types of its parameters.

```
type MyFunction = (a: number, b: string) => boolean;

type MyFunctionParameters = Parameters<MyFunction>;
// MyFunctionParameters is [number, string]
```

keyof operator

The keyof operator is used to produce a union type of all known, enumerable property names of a given type. It allows you to work with the keys (property names) of an object type in a type-safe manner.

In this example, keyof Point produces the union type "x" | "y", which means that you can use the PointKeys type to represent either the string literal "x" or "y".

```typescript
type Point = { x: number; y: number };

type PointKeys = keyof Point;
// PointKeys is "x" | "y"
```

In this example, the getCoordinate function takes a Point object and a key (using keyof Point) and returns the corresponding coordinate value. The TypeScript compiler ensures that you can only pass valid keys ("x" or "y") to the function.

```typescript
type Point = { x: number; y: number };

function getCoordinate(point: Point, axis: keyof Point): number {
    return point[axis];
}

const myPoint: Point = { x: 1, y: 2 };

const xCoordinate = getCoordinate(myPoint, "x"); // valid
const zCoordinate = getCoordinate(myPoint, "z"); // error: //
Argument of type '"z"' is not assignable to parameter
// of type 'keyof Point'
```

RxJS

RxJS, short for Reactive Extensions for JavaScript, is a library for reactive programming using Observables, which are a proposed standard for managing asynchronous data streams. RxJS provides a functional programming style for dealing with asynchronous data streams and handling events. It is heavily inspired by the concept of Observables from the ReactiveX project, which originated in the .NET world.

RxJS is widely used in JavaScript and TypeScript applications, especially in environments where managing asynchronous data flows and event handling is crucial, such as web development, real-time applications, and reactive programming paradigms. It's commonly used with frameworks like Angular, React, and Vue.js to handle asynchronous operations and state management.

Some key concepts in RxJS include:

Observable: Represents a collection of values or events over time. Observables can emit zero or more events, and consumers can subscribe to these events.

Observer: A consumer of values emitted by an Observable. It is an object with three optional callback functions: next(), error(), and complete(), which respectively handle emitted values, errors, and the completion of the Observable stream.

Operators: Functions that can be used to manipulate the data emitted by Observables. Operators are used to transform, filter, combine, and perform various operations on the data streams.

Subscription: Represents the execution of an Observable. Subscriptions are created by calling the subscribe() method on an Observable and can be used to unsubscribe from receiving further values.

Subject: A special type of Observable that allows both emitting and subscribing to events. Subjects are useful for multicast scenarios where multiple subscribers want to listen to the same stream of events.

Install RxJS: `npm i rxjs`

Observable

```javascript
import { Observable } from "rxjs";

const observable = new Observable(observer => {
    // async logic 1
    setTimeout(() => {
        observer.next('Hello');
    }, 1000);

    // async logic 2
    setTimeout(() => {
        observer.next('World');
    }, 2000);

    // Complete the observable after async logic
    setTimeout(() => {
        observer.complete();
    }, 3000);
});

observable.subscribe({
    next: (value) => console.log(value),
    complete: () => console.log('Observable1 completed'),
});

observable.subscribe({
    next: (value) => console.log(value),
    complete: () => console.log('Observable2 completed'),
});

/*
Outputs:
Hello
Hello
World
World
Observable1 completed
Observable2 completed
*/
```

Here, we're creating a new Observable instance. The constructor of the Observable class takes a function as an argument. This function receives an observer object, which is used to emit values and handle completion of the Observable.

Inside the function passed to the Observable constructor:

We use setTimeout to simulate asynchronous operations.

After 1 second, we call observer.next('Hello'), which emits the value 'Hello'.

After 2 seconds, we call observer.next('World'), which emits the value 'World'.

After 3 seconds, we call observer.complete() to indicate that the Observable has completed emitting values.

The subscribe method is used to create a subscription to an Observable. Subscriptions are the mechanism through which Observables can be executed and values emitted by them can be received. The subscribe method takes an Observer object or individual callback functions as arguments.

We subscribe twice to the Observable instance observable. We pass an observer object to the subscribe method, which defines how to handle emitted values (next) and completion (complete).

The next function logs each emitted value to the console.

The complete function logs a message when the Observable completes emitting values.

So, in summary, this code creates an Observable that emits the values 'Hello' and 'World' asynchronously using setTimeout, and then completes after emitting both values. It demonstrates how to handle asynchronous operations within an Observable and how to subscribe to it to consume the emitted values.

Observer

Observer is an interface that consists of three callback functions: next, error, and complete. Observers are used to subscribe to Observables and receive notifications of emitted values, errors, and completion. Here's a breakdown of each callback function:

next: The next callback is called when an Observable emits a value. It receives the emitted value as an argument.

error: The error callback is called when an error occurs during the execution of the Observable. It receives the error object as an argument.

complete: The complete callback is called when the Observable completes successfully, meaning it has emitted all its values and won't emit any more. It doesn't receive any arguments.

```
import { Observable } from 'rxjs';

const observable = new Observable(observer => {
    observer.next(1);
    observer.next(2);
    observer.error(3);
    observer.complete();
});

const observer = {
    next: (value: any) => console.log('Next:', value),
    error: (error: any) => console.error('Error:', error),
    complete: () => console.log('Completed'),
};

observable.subscribe(observer);
/*
Outputs:
Next: 1
Next: 2
Error: 3
*/
```

You subscribe to the Observable using the Observer object observer.

When the Observable emits values, the next callback of the Observer is called, logging the value to the console.

When the Observable emits an error, the error callback of the Observer is called, logging the error to the console.

Since an error occurs in the Observable sequence, the complete callback is not executed.

Unsubscribe

The unsubscribe method is used to stop receiving notifications from an Observable. Subscriptions to Observables are meant to be canceled when they are no longer needed to prevent memory leaks and unnecessary processing. The unsubscribe method is called on a Subscription object returned by the subscribe method.

```javascript
import { Observable } from 'rxjs';

const observable = new Observable(observer => {
    // Emit values over time
    const intervalId = setInterval(() => {
        observer.next('Hello');
    }, 1000);

    // Cleanup logic when unsubscribed
    return () => {
        clearInterval(intervalId);
        console.log('Observable unsubscribed');
    };
});

const subscription = observable.subscribe(value => {
    console.log(value);
});

// Unsubscribe after 5 seconds
setTimeout(() => {
    subscription.unsubscribe();
}, 5000);
```

We create an Observable that emits the value 'Hello' every second using setInterval.

The subscribe method is used to start listening to the Observable, and it returns a Subscription object.

We use setTimeout to call unsubscribe on the Subscription object after 5 seconds.

After unsubscribing, the cleanup logic defined inside the Observable's creation function (the returned function) is executed, which clears the interval and logs a message.

By unsubscribing from the Observable, we stop receiving notifications from it and release any resources associated with it. This is important for managing resources efficiently, especially in long-running applications.

Observable vs Promise

Observable and Promises are both concepts used in asynchronous programming, particularly in JavaScript. Here's a brief overview of each:

Promise

A Promise represents a value which may be available now, or in the future, or never.

It's a single value that may be available immediately, or might be resolved at some point in the future, or never get resolved.

Promises have states: pending, fulfilled, or rejected.

Promises are generally used for handling asynchronous operations, such as fetching data from a server or reading a file asynchronously.

Promises are essentially a pattern for asynchronous programming, allowing you to attach callbacks to handle success or failure once the asynchronous operation is completed.

```javascript
const myPromise = new Promise((resolve, reject) => {
  // Asynchronous operation
  setTimeout(() => {
    resolve('Operation completed');
  }, 1000);
});

myPromise.then((result) => {
  console.log(result); // Output: Operation completed
}).catch((error) => {
  console.error(error);
});
```

Observable

An Observable is a data source that emits values over time.

It represents a stream of data that can be observed over time.

Observables are more powerful than Promises because they can emit multiple values over time.

Observables can be used for handling asynchronous operations just like Promises, but they offer more features such as cancellation and composition.

```javascript
import { Observable } from 'rxjs';

const myObservable = new Observable(observer => {
  // Emit a value after 1 second
  setTimeout(() => {
    observer.next('Value emitted after 1 second');
  }, 1000);
});

myObservable.subscribe(value => {
  console.log(value); // Output: Value emitted after 1 sec
});
```

In summary, Promises are simpler and suitable for handling single asynchronous operations, while Observables are more powerful and suitable for handling streams of data over time.

Operators

RxJS operators are functions that can be used to manipulate the data emitted by observables. They allow you to create complex data processing pipelines by transforming, filtering, combining, or aggregating the data emitted by observables. RxJS provides a rich set of operators for various purposes.

RxJS operators encompass a wide array of functionalities. Let's explore some of them.

Creation Operators

Creation Operators are a set of operators used to create Observables from various data sources or events.

of

The of operator is used to create an Observable that emits a sequence of values. It accepts a variable number of arguments, each representing a value to be emitted by the Observable.

```javascript
import { of } from 'rxjs';

of(1, 2, 3).subscribe({
    next: value => console.log(value)
});

/*
Outputs:
1
2
3
*/

of([1, 2, 3]).subscribe({
    next: value => console.log(value)
});

// Outputs: [1,2,3]
```

from

Converts various other data sources and structures into Observables.

```
import { from } from 'rxjs';

from([1, 2, 3]).subscribe({
    next: value => console.log(value)
});

/*
Outputs:
1
2
3
*/
```

of operator is used to emit a fixed set of values provided as arguments, while from operator is used to convert various data sources into Observables.

interval

Emits sequential numbers at specified intervals.

```
import { interval } from 'rxjs';

interval(1000).subscribe({ // Emits every 1 second
    next: value => console.log(value)
});

/*
Outputs:
0
1
2
.
.
∞
*/
```

range

Emits a sequence of numbers within a specified range.

```
import { range } from 'rxjs';

range(1, 3).subscribe({
    next: value => console.log(value)
});

// Outputs:
// 1
// 2
// 3
```

timer

Emits a single value after a specified delay, and then completes.

```
import { timer } from 'rxjs';

timer(2000).subscribe({ // Emits after 2 seconds
    next: value => console.log(value)
});

// Outputs: 0
```

iif

iif operator conditionally subscribes to one of two Observables based on a condition.

```
import { iif, of } from 'rxjs';

const condition = true;
iif(() => condition, of('True'), of('False')).subscribe({
    next: value => console.log(value)});

//Outputs: true
```

Join Operators

Join Operators are used to create Observables by combining multiple sources of data or events. They allow you to merge, combine, or join streams of data emitted by different Observables.

pipe

The pipe function is used to chain multiple operators together to create a data processing pipeline. It allows you to apply a series of transformations, filtering, mapping, or other operations to the data emitted by an Observable.

```
import { of } from 'rxjs';
import { map, filter } from 'rxjs/operators';

const source$ = of(1, 2, 3, 4, 5);

source$.pipe(
   filter(x => x % 2 === 0), // Filter out odd numbers
   map(x => x * 10)          // Multiply each even number by 10
   )
   .subscribe(result => {
       console.log(result);
   });

// Output:
// 20
// 40
```

The pipe method takes an arbitrary number of operators as arguments. Each operator is a pure function that transforms the data emitted by the observable. When you call pipe on an observable, it returns a new observable with the operators applied to it.

combineLatest

The concat operator used to combine multiple observables into one by sequentially emitting their values, one after the other, in the order they are provided. It subscribes to each observable one by one, only moving to the next observable once the current one completes.

```
import { of, concat } from 'rxjs';

const source1$ = of('A', 'B');
const source2$ = of(1, 2);

const concatenated$ = concat(source1$, source2$);

concatenated$.subscribe(value => {
    console.log(value);
});
// Outputs:
// A
// B
// 1
// 2
```

In this example, concat subscribes to source1$ first and emits its values ('A', 'B') sequentially. Once source1$ completes, concat then subscribes to source2$ and emits its values (1, 2) sequentially.

The convention of appending a dollar sign ($) to variable names is often used to indicate that the variable represents an Observable. This naming convention helps developers easily identify Observables within their codebase.

forkJoin

forkJoin is an operator used to combine multiple observables into a single observable that emits an array of the last values emitted by the source observables, once all of them have emitted at least one value, and then completes. It waits for all observables to complete before emitting the array.

```
import { of, forkJoin } from 'rxjs';

const source1$ = of('A', 'B');
const source2$ = of(1, 2);

forkJoin({
    source1: source1$,
    source2: source2$
}).subscribe(result => {
    console.log(result);
});

// Output:
// {source1: 'B', source2: 2}
```

In this example, forkJoin waits for both source1$ and source2$ to complete and then emits an array containing the last values emitted by each observable. Since both observables emit three values each, it takes the last emitted value from each observable ('B' from source1$ and 2 from source2$) and emits them as an object.

merge

merge is an operator used to combine multiple observables into one observable that emits all the values from all the source observables, regardless of the order they are emitted in. This means that values from any of the source observables can be emitted concurrently.

```javascript
import { of, merge } from 'rxjs';

const source1$ = of('A', 'B');
const source2$ = of(1, 2);

const merged$ = merge(source1$, source2$);

merged$.subscribe(value => {
    console.log(value);
});

// Output:
// A
// B
// 1
// 2
```

mergeAll

The mergeAll operator is used to flatten an observable of observables into a single observable sequence by merging all inner observables emitted by the source observable concurrently.

```
import { of } from 'rxjs';
import { mergeAll } from 'rxjs/operators';

// Create an observable of observables
const source$ = of(
    of(1, 2),
    of(3, 4)
);

// Use mergeAll to flatten the observable of observables
const flattened$ = source$.pipe(mergeAll());

flattened$.subscribe(value => {
    console.log(value);
});

// Output:
// 1
// 2
// 3
// 4
```

In this example, source$ emits three inner observables: of(1, 2) and of(3,4). When you apply mergeAll, it subscribes to each inner observable concurrently. As soon as any inner observable emits a value, that value is emitted on the output observable. This results in a single observable sequence that emits all values from all inner observables, regardless of the order they are emitted.

mergeMap

mergeMap (formerly known as flatMap) allows you to perform a projection on each item emitted by a source observable and then flatten these projected inner observables into a single observable stream. It is often used when you have observables that emit other observables, and you want to merge the emissions from all the inner observables into a single stream.

```
import { of } from 'rxjs';
import { mergeMap } from 'rxjs/operators';

// Let's say we have an observable emitting numbers
const source$ = of(1, 2, 3);

// We'll use mergeMap to map each emitted number to an
// observable that emits that number multiplied by 10
source$.pipe(
    mergeMap(num => of(num * 10))
).subscribe(result => {
    console.log(result);
});
// Output:
// 10
// 20
// 30
```

In this example, mergeMap transforms each emitted number into a new observable that emits the number multiplied by 10. mergeMap then merges these inner observables into a single stream. The output will be the flattened emissions from all the inner observables.

partition

The partition operator is used to split a source observable into two separate observables based on a predicate function. It takes a source observable and a predicate function as input and returns an array containing two observables: one that emits values for which the predicate function returns true, and another that emits values for which the predicate function returns false.

```
import { of, partition } from 'rxjs';

const source$ = of(1, 2, 3, 4);

const [even$, odd$] = partition(source$, value => value % 2 ===
0);

even$.subscribe(value => {
    console.log(`Even: ${value}`);
});

odd$.subscribe(value => {
    console.log(`Odd: ${value}`);
});

// Output:
// Even: 2
// Even: 4
// Odd: 1
// Odd: 3
```

In this example, partition is used to split the source$ observable into two observables: even$ and odd$. even$ emits values that satisfy the predicate function (value % 2 === 0), i.e., even numbers, while odd$ emits values that do not satisfy the predicate function, i.e., odd numbers.

race

The race operator is used to race multiple source observables against each other, and emit the first value emitted by any of the source observables. It essentially competes among multiple observables, and as soon as one of them emits a value or completes, race emits that value or completion event, and then unsubscribes from all other source observables.

```
import { race, interval, of } from 'rxjs';
import { take } from 'rxjs/operators';

const source1$ = of(1, 2);
const source2$ = of(3, 4);

race(source1$, source2$).subscribe(value => {
    console.log(value);
});

// Output:
// 1
// 2
```

When you run this code, the race operator will emit the first value that is emitted by either source1$ or source2$. Since both observables emit their values synchronously and source1$ emits '1' first followed by '2', '1' will be the first value emitted and then '2'. As soon as '1' is emitted, the race operator completes and the subscription is unsubscribed, so '2' is not emitted.

zip

The zip operator is used to combine the values emitted by multiple observables into arrays, emitting the arrays only when each observable has emitted a new value. The emitted arrays will contain the latest value from each of the source observables, and the number of emitted arrays is equal to the number of values emitted by the shortest observable.

```
import { zip, of } from 'rxjs';

const source1$ = of(1);
const source2$ = of(2, 3);
const source3$ = of(4, 5, 6);

zip(source1$, source2$, source3$).subscribe(values => {
    console.log(values);
});

// Output:
// [1, 2, 4]
```

In this example, zip combines the values emitted by source1$, source2$, and source3$ into arrays. Since source1$ emits only one value (1), source2$ emits two values (2 and 3), and source3$ emits three values (4, 5, and 6), the resulting arrays emitted by zip will contain one value from each observable.

However, because source1$ completes after emitting its single value, and source2$ and source3$ continue emitting values, zip will complete after emitting the first array. The emission of arrays stops once the shortest observable (source1$) completes.

concatAll

The concatAll operator is used to flatten an observable of observables into a single observable sequence by sequentially concatenating all inner observables emitted by the source observable.

```javascript
import { of } from 'rxjs';
import { concatAll } from 'rxjs/operators';

const source$ = of(
    of(1, 2, 3),
    of(4, 5, 6),
);

const flattened$ = source$.pipe(concatAll());

flattened$.subscribe(value => {
    console.log(value);
});
// Output:
// 1
// 2
// 3
// 4
// 5
// 6
```

In this example, source$ emits three inner observables: of(1, 2, 3) and of(4, 5, 6), When you apply concatAll, it subscribes to each inner observable sequentially. It waits for each inner observable to complete before subscribing to the next one. This results in a single observable sequence that emits all values in the order they are emitted by the inner observables.

Transformation Operators

Transformation operators are used to transform or manipulate the data emitted by observables. These operators allow you to modify the emitted values before they are consumed by subscribers.

map

The map operator is used to transform the items emitted by an observable into a new form. It applies a given function to each item emitted by the source observable and emits the result.

```
import { of } from 'rxjs';
import { map } from 'rxjs/operators';

const source$ = of(1, 2, 3);

// Apply map operator to double each emitted number
const doubled$ = source$.pipe(
    map(value => value * 2)
);

doubled$.subscribe(doubledValue => {
    console.log(doubledValue);
});
// Outputs:
// 2
// 4
// 6
```

In this example, we have an observable source$ emitting numbers from 1 to 3. We use the map operator to transform each emitted value by doubling it. The resulting observable doubled$ emits the transformed values (2, 4, 6).

groupBy

The groupBy operator is used to group the items emitted by an observable into separate observables based on a specified key selector function. It creates an observable group for each unique key and emits these groups as higher-order observables.

```
import { of } from 'rxjs';
import { groupBy, mergeMap, toArray } from 'rxjs/operators';

const source$ = of(
    { id: 1, name: 'Eldar' },
    { id: 2, name: 'David' },
    { id: 3, name: 'Eldar' },
);

const grouped$ = source$.pipe(
    groupBy(obj => obj.name),
    mergeMap(group => group.pipe(toArray()))
);

grouped$.subscribe(group => {
    console.log(JSON.stringify(group));
});

// Outputs:
// [{"id":1,"name":"Eldar"},{"id":3,"name":"Eldar"}]
// [{"id":2,"name":"David"}]
```

In this example, we have an observable source$ emitting a list of objects with id and name properties. We use the groupBy operator to group these objects by the name property. Each unique name will create a separate observable group.

Then, we use mergeMap to flatten the higher-order observables emitted by groupBy and toArray to collect all items in each group into an array.

Filtering Operators

Filtering operators are used to selectively emit values from an observable based on certain criteria. These operators allow you to control which values are passed downstream to subscribers.

filter

The filter operator is used to selectively emit values from an observable based on a provided predicate function. It allows you to filter out values that don't meet a specific condition, passing only those that do meet the condition downstream to subscribers.

```
import { of } from 'rxjs';
import { filter } from 'rxjs/operators';

const source$ = of(1, 2, 3, 4);

// Use filter to emit only even numbers
const filtered$ = source$.pipe(
    filter(number => number % 2 === 0)
);

filtered$.subscribe(filteredNumber => {
    console.log(filteredNumber);
});

// Output:
// 2
// 4
```

In this example, the filter operator is applied to the source$ observable. It filters out odd numbers by checking if each number emitted by the source observable is even (number % 2 === 0). Only the even numbers pass through the filter and are emitted downstream.

first/last

The first and last operators are used to extract the first and last values emitted by an observable, respectively.

```
import { of } from 'rxjs';
import { first, last } from 'rxjs/operators';

const source$ = of(1, 2, 3);

source$.pipe(
    first() // Emit only the first value
).subscribe(
    value => console.log(value),
);
// Output: 1

source$.pipe(
    last() // Emit only the first value
).subscribe(
    value => console.log(value),
);

// Output: 3
```

skip/take

The skip and take operators are used to control the number of values emitted by an observable.

The skip operator skips the first n values emitted by the source observable and then emits the remaining values.

The take operator emits only the first n values emitted by the source observable and then completes.

```
import { of } from 'rxjs';
import { skip, take } from 'rxjs/operators';

const source$ = of(1, 2, 3, 4, 5);

source$.pipe(
    skip(1), // Skip the first value
    take(2) // Take the first 2 values
).subscribe(
    value => console.log(value)
);

// Output:
// 2
// 3
```

skip(1): This operator skips the first value emitted by source$. So, the value 1 is skipped.

take(2): This operator takes the next two values emitted by source$. The values 2 and 3 are emitted.

skipLast/takeLast

The skipLast and takeLast operators are used to skip or take the last n values emitted by the source observable, respectively.

```
import { of } from 'rxjs';
import { skipLast, takeLast } from 'rxjs/operators';

const source$ = of(1, 2, 3, 4, 5);

source$.pipe(
    skipLast(2), // Skip the last 2 values
    takeLast(2) // take the last 2 values

).subscribe(
    value => console.log(value)
);

// Output:
// 2
// 3
```

skipLast(2): This operator skips the last two values emitted by source$, which are 4 and 5.

takeLast(2): This operator takes the last two values emitted by source$, which are 2 and 3, skipping the previously skipped values.

So, the final emitted values are 2 and 3, which is what you see in the output.

Subjects

A subject is a special type of observable that allows both the ability to subscribe to it and to manually push values into it. Subjects act as both observers and observables, which makes them useful for multicasting values to multiple subscribers. There are several types of subjects:

Subject: A basic type of subject that allows both subscribing to it and pushing values into it directly using its next() method.

BehaviorSubject: This type of subject requires an initial value and always emits the most recent value to new subscribers immediately upon subscription. It retains the latest value pushed to it and emits it to any new subscribers.

ReplaySubject: This subject type records a specific number of values and replays them to new subscribers. You can specify how many values to replay when creating it.

AsyncSubject: This subject only emits the last value emitted by the source observable (or the final value upon completion) only after the source completes. If the source never completes, AsyncSubject will never emit a value.

Subjects are commonly used in scenarios where you want to multicast values to multiple subscribers and where you need more control over when and what values are emitted. They are particularly useful in cases such as event handling, data sharing among components, or creating observable-based APIs. However, they should be used with caution as they break the unidirectional data flow principle in reactive programming and can lead to complex data flow patterns if not used carefully.

Subject

```javascript
import { Subject } from 'rxjs';

// Create a subject
const subject = new Subject();

// Subscribe to the subject
subject.subscribe({
    next: value => console.log('Observer A:', value)
});

// Push value into the subject
subject.next(1); // Output: Observer A: 1

// Subscribe another observer
subject.subscribe({
    next: value => console.log('Observer B:', value)
});

// Push another value
subject.next(2); // Output: Observer A: 2
                 //         Observer B: 2
```

You create a new instance of Subject called subject.

You subscribe an observer to subject, labeled as "Observer A". This observer logs the values it receives.

You push a value 1 into the subject using subject.next(1).

Observer A logs the received value 1.

You subscribe another observer to subject, labeled as "Observer B".

You push another value 2 into the subject using subject.next(2).

Both Observer A and Observer B receive and log the value 2 because they subscribed after the value was pushed.

BehaviorSubject

```javascript
import { BehaviorSubject } from 'rxjs';

// Create a BehaviorSubject with initial value
const behaviorSubject = new BehaviorSubject(0);

// Subscribe to the BehaviorSubject
behaviorSubject.subscribe({
    next: value => console.log('Observer A:', value)
});

// Push value into the BehaviorSubject
behaviorSubject.next(1); // Output: Observer A: 1

// Subscribe another observer
behaviorSubject.subscribe({
    next: value => console.log('Observer B:', value)
});

// Push another value
behaviorSubject.next(2); // Output: Observer A: 2
                         //         Observer B: 2
```

You create a new instance of BehaviorSubject called behaviorSubject with an initial value of 0.

You subscribe an observer to behaviorSubject, labeled as "Observer A". This observer logs the values it receives.

You push a value 1 into the behaviorSubject using behaviorSubject.next(1).

Observer A logs the received value 1.

You subscribe another observer to behaviorSubject, labeled as "Observer B".

Since BehaviorSubject stores the most recent value and emits it immediately to new subscribers upon subscription, Observer B receives the latest value, which is 1. It logs 1.

You push another value 2 into the behaviorSubject using behaviorSubject.next(2).

Both Observer A and Observer B receive and log the new value 2.

ReplaySubject

```javascript
import { ReplaySubject } from 'rxjs';

// Create a ReplaySubject with buffer size 2
const replaySubject = new ReplaySubject(2);

// Push values into the ReplaySubject
replaySubject.next(1);
replaySubject.next(2);
replaySubject.next(3);

// Subscribe to the ReplaySubject
replaySubject.subscribe({
    next: value => console.log('Observer:', value)
});

// Output: Observer: 2,
//         Observer: 3
```

You create a new instance of ReplaySubject called replaySubject with a buffer size of 2. This means it will replay the last 2 values to new subscribers.

You push values 1, 2, and 3 into the replaySubject using replaySubject.next().

Since the buffer size is 2, replaySubject will only keep the last 2 values, which are 2 and 3.

You subscribe an observer to replaySubject, which logs the values it receives.

The observer receives and logs the buffered values, which are 2 and 3.

This demonstrates how ReplaySubject in RxJS replays a specified number of buffered values to new subscribers. In this case, it replays the last 2 values (2 and 3).

AsyncSubject

```javascript
import { AsyncSubject } from 'rxjs';

// Create an AsyncSubject
const asyncSubject = new AsyncSubject();

// Push values into the AsyncSubject
asyncSubject.next(1);
asyncSubject.next(2);
asyncSubject.next(3);

// Subscribe to the AsyncSubject
asyncSubject.subscribe({
    next: value => console.log('Observer:', value)
});

asyncSubject.complete(); // Complete the subject

// Output: Observer: 3
```

You create a new instance of AsyncSubject called asyncSubject.

You push values 1, 2, and 3 into the asyncSubject using asyncSubject.next().

These values are stored internally, but they are not emitted yet because AsyncSubject only emits the last value (or only the completion signal if there are no values) after it's completed.

You subscribe an observer to asyncSubject, which logs the values it receives.

You complete the asyncSubject using asyncSubject.complete().

Since the asyncSubject is completed, it emits the last value it received, which is 3, to the subscriber.

The observer receives and logs the emitted value, which is 3.

Scheduler

A scheduler is an object that controls when a subscription starts and when notifications (such as next, error, and complete) are delivered to observers. It abstracts away the notion of time and allows you to specify whether operations should be synchronous or asynchronous and how they should be scheduled.

Schedulers are particularly useful for managing concurrency, timing, and controlling the execution context of observables. RxJS provides several built-in schedulers, each with its own characteristics:

ImmediateScheduler: Schedules tasks synchronously. It executes tasks as soon as they are scheduled without any delay.

AsapScheduler: Schedules tasks asynchronously but as soon as possible, typically after the current synchronous code has finished executing.

AsyncScheduler: Schedules tasks asynchronously using setTimeout or setInterval. It's used for non-blocking operations and introduces a minimal delay.

QueueScheduler: Schedules tasks serially using a queue, ensuring that tasks are executed in the order they are scheduled. It's useful for scenarios where ordering is important.

AnimationFrameScheduler: Schedules tasks to be executed in sync with the browser's animation loop, typically at a rate of 60 frames per second.

VirtualTimeScheduler: A scheduler for testing observables with time-dependent operators in a virtual time environment. It allows you to simulate the passage of time without waiting for real time to elapse.

Schedulers can be specified when creating observables or when using operators that involve time, such as delay, throttleTime, debounceTime, etc. They provide control over how and when operations are executed, making RxJS suitable for a wide range of applications, including reactive UIs, asynchronous data processing, and testing.

ImmediateScheduler

```
import { of, asyncScheduler } from 'rxjs';

console.log('Before of()');
of(1, 2, 3, asyncScheduler).subscribe(value =>
console.log(value));
console.log('After of()');
// Output:
// Before of()
// After of()
// 1
// 2
// 3
```

In this example, of() operator is used to create an observable emitting values 1, 2, and 3. When using asyncScheduler, values are emitted synchronously, but they are enqueued in the microtask queue. Hence, "Before of()" and "After of()" are logged before the values.

AsapScheduler

```
import { asyncScheduler, asapScheduler } from 'rxjs';

console.log('Before asapScheduler');
asyncScheduler.schedule(() => console.log('Inside scheduler'));
asapScheduler.schedule(() => console.log('Inside scheduler'));
console.log('After asapScheduler');
// Output:
// Before asapScheduler
// After asapScheduler
// Inside asapScheduler
// Inside asyncScheduler
```

asapScheduler schedules tasks to run asynchronously but as soon as possible. In the example, "Before asapScheduler" and "After asapScheduler" are logged before the scheduled tasks. However, the task scheduled with asapScheduler is executed before the task scheduled with asyncScheduler.

AsyncScheduler

```
import { asyncScheduler } from 'rxjs';

console.log('Before Scheduler');
asyncScheduler.schedule(() => console.log('Inside Scheduler'));
console.log('After Scheduler');
// Output:
// Before Scheduler
// After Scheduler
// Inside Scheduler
```

asyncScheduler schedules tasks to run asynchronously. In this example, "Before asyncScheduler" and "After asyncScheduler" are logged before the scheduled task. The task is executed asynchronously, so "Inside asyncScheduler" is logged afterward.

QueueScheduler

```
import { queueScheduler, of } from 'rxjs';

console.log('Before queueScheduler');
of(1, 2, 3, queueScheduler).subscribe(value =>
console.log(value));
console.log('After queueScheduler');
// Output:
// Before queueScheduler
// 1
// 2
// 3
// After queueScheduler
```

queueScheduler schedules tasks to run serially. In this example, "Before queueScheduler" is logged before the values, and "After queueScheduler" is logged after the values indicating the synchronous nature. The values are emitted in the order they were scheduled.

AnimationFrameScheduler

```
import { animationFrameScheduler } from 'rxjs';

console.log('Before animationFrameScheduler');
animationFrameScheduler.schedule(() =>
                console.log('Inside animationFrameScheduler'));
console.log('After animationFrameScheduler');

// Output:
// Before animationFrameScheduler
// After animationFrameScheduler
// Inside animationFrameScheduler
```

animationFrameScheduler schedules tasks to run in sync with the browser's animation loop. In this example, "Before animationFrameScheduler" and "After animationFrameScheduler" are logged before the scheduled task. The task is executed in sync with the animation frame, so "Inside animationFrameScheduler" is logged afterward.

VirtualTimeScheduler

```javascript
import { VirtualTimeScheduler, of } from 'rxjs';
import { delay, tap } from 'rxjs/operators';

// Create a VirtualTimeScheduler instance
const scheduler = new VirtualTimeScheduler();

// Emit values 1, 2, 3 with delays of 1000ms between each using
// VirtualTimeScheduler
console.log('Before scheduling');
of(1, 2, 3).pipe(
    delay(1000, scheduler), // Use VirtualTimeScheduler for
                            // delaying emissions
    tap(value => console.log(`Emitting ${value}`))
).subscribe();
console.log('After scheduling');

// Advance the scheduler's clock by 1500ms
scheduler.flush();

// Output:
// Before scheduling
// After scheduling
// Emitting 1
// Emitting 2
// Emitting 3
```

We create an instance of VirtualTimeScheduler named scheduler.

We create an observable using of() emitting values 1, 2, and 3.

We apply a delay of 1000 milliseconds between each emission using the delay operator, specifying scheduler as the scheduler to use.

We subscribe to the observable. Since we're using VirtualTimeScheduler, no actual time is elapsed at this point.

We call scheduler.flush() to advance the scheduler's clock by 1500 milliseconds. This simulates the passage of time in a controlled manner.

As a result, the delayed emissions are processed, and we see the log messages indicating the emitted values after the specified delays.